G000291521

NEW ZEALAND SLANG DICTIONARY

Compiled by
Harry Orsman and Des Hurley

REED

INTRODUCTION

Traditionally, New Zealand slang has been a bit of a fancy mixture, something of a *bitser*, as it would say itself. Some is 'Antipodean', that is, 'common Australasian'; some has been shared with seamen (*doctor*, an old-fashioned word for a sheep-station cook, for example); some taken over from English dialect (*skerrick*); and some from Maori (the old-fashioned *hoot*, money, from Maori *utu*, compensation).

Much of yesterday's slang has moved out to make room for

tomorrow's. For example, as a
young man in World War I my
father, a third generation Kiwi,
could recite with relish:

'I've lorst me former joy in
    gettin' shick,
Or 'eadin' browns; I 'aven't got
    the 'eart
To word a tom; an', square an' all,
    I'm sick of that cheap tart
'Oo chucks 'er carkis at a
    feller's 'ead.
'An mauls 'im . . . Ar! I wish't that I
    wus dead!'

It is almost incomprehensible
now; *brown,* a penny, *tom,* a girl
are well gone, and *chat up* has
replaced *word.*

So things change, and with satellite TV and Aussie soap-opera it's now sometimes hard to tell who's up to what and with whose burnt stick. Be that as it may, what follows is for the most part New Zealand popular speech, the call of the contemporary Kiwi, with a few oldies thrown in — as is often the fate of oldies.

A

aftermatch function
    a drinking session after a
    sporting event

**all cock and ribs like a
musterer's dog**
    very skinny

all hands and the cook
    everybody

amber, the amber fluid
    beer

anklebiter
    a toddler

ante up
    come to light with, pay up

appetite like a fantail
little or no appetite

arvo
afternoon

away laughing
indicating something
successfully completed: 'Hadlee
gets a century and we're away
laughing.'

away with the fairies
fey, 'not with it'

HA HA HA

HA HA

HA

B

bach or batch
a hut or living quarters fit only for a bachelor; a holiday cottage

backbone of the country
the farming community

banjo
a shovel; occasionally a leg of mutton

barbie
a barbecue

barrack
to tease, to rib

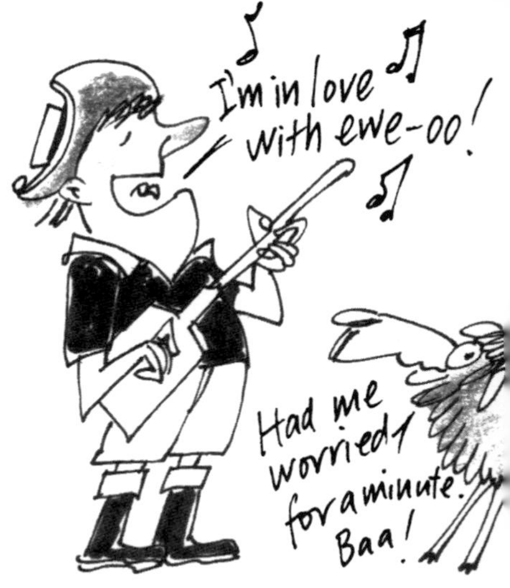
I'm in love with ewe-oo!
Had me worried for a minute. Baa!

barrack for

to support vociferously: 'Every time we barracked for our basketball team it won.'

barracouta loaf

a long, raised-crust loaf: from a fancied resemblance to the long, lean, rough-backed barracouta fish

bash

a drinking party or spree

battler

one who struggles against adversity or has to work hard for a living

beaut
something or someone fine or outstanding; often used ironically: 'He's a beaut: never pays his share.'

beautee
an exclamation of delight

beer sandwich
beer in lieu of lunch

bend the elbow
to have a few drinks (often more realistically *wet the elbow*)

berkers
violent or crazy (from berserk)

bible-basher
a clergyman, or enthusiastic lapsed agnostic

biddy-bid
a burr-bearing plant (from Maori *piripiri*)

big bickies
big money, large sums

big note
to announce wealth ostentatiously (as by flashing $100 bills)

big smoke
the town or city

big spit
a muted technicolour yawn

bikie
a member of a motorbike gang

binder
a solid meal

bitser
a mongrel dog, a machine, made of 'bitsan' pieces, etc.

block
a gang rape

blowie
a blowfly

bludge
to cadge

bludger
a cadger; one who lives off others, hence, a term of abuse: originally *bludgeoner*, a prostitute's pimp

blue (noun)
a mistake; a fight or brawl

blue (verb)
  to spend all one's money

bluey
  (formerly) a summons to court;
  a traffic ticket; also a swag:
  one's belongings rolled in a
  blanket for easy carrying

bodgie
  a subcultural male of the 1950s

bomb
  an aged motor vehicle

bonzer
  outstanding, fine, beaut

boob, boob tatt
  prison; a skin tattoo done in
  prison

boohai, the boohai

a remote district or area, the 'sticks' or backblocks; *up the boohai,* very much awry. As the poet Edward Lear may have said:
'On the coast of Coromandel where the magic pumpkins blow Lived a jughead with a handle of 'Bonger Boohai Joe.'

boomer

something large or outstanding of its class

boong(a)

an offensive word for a coloured person

booze artist

a heavy drinker

boozeroo
  a pub; a drinking session

borough council
  a small corporation

bot
  a germ or bug; a sickness:
  'To catch the bot.'

box of birds
  fine, happy, going well

brewer's goitre
  a beer-gut or pot gut

brown-eye
  the naked arse revealed as a
  sign of contempt for the
  revealee(s)

brummy
  shoddy: from Brummagen, a
  name for Birmingham

Buckley's (chance)
  no or little chance (of success)

buggerlugs, buggylugs
  a term of endearment

bull-artist
  a practised liar

bulldust
  nonsense

bully for you!
  an ironic or derisive exclamation

bung
  bankrupt; broken, out of order

bushwhacker
a bushfeller

bust one's boiler
to exert oneself vigorously; to collapse through over-exertion

buster
old-fashioned name for a country newspaper. (See also *southerly buster*)

busy as a one-armed paperhanger
very busy (often in a haphazard way)

C

captain cooker
  a wild pig

cardie
  a cardigan

cast
  immobilised (e.g. through
  drunkenness) as of a sheep
  unable to get to its feet

chateau cardboard
  an up-market name for wine in
  a cask

chews
  sweets, lollies

chiack, shiack
  to tease; to throw off at

chocker
completely full

chook
a fowl or chicken; *to act like a headless chook*, to behave hysterically

chuck a wobblie
to have a fit of hysteria or faintness

chuddy, chutty
chewing-gum

chunder
(to) vomit

clobbering machine
> a fanciful name for the Kiwi habit of cutting outstanding people down to size; a reaper of tall poppies

cob(ber)
> a mate, especially as 'Me old cob'

cockabully
> a small freshwater fish: from Maori *kokopu(ru)*

cockie
> a farmer (formerly and usually on a small-holding; also *cow-cockie*, a dairy farmer, *sheep-cockie*, a pastoral farmer)

cockie's joy
  golden syrup or treacle

coconut
  an offensive word for a Pacific Islander

come a thud
  to fail in an enterprise

cookshop
  the cookhouse of a workman's camp

corker
  fine, beaut

corporation
  a protruding stomach

cot-case
  a person confined to bed through illness or injury

cow-spanker
a dairy-farmer

crook
> ill; awry or broken; angry: as
> *feel crook*, ill; *go crook (at)*, to
> scold; *put one in crook with (a
> boss, etc.)*, to put someone in ill
> favour with

cunning as a shithouse rat
> very cunning

cut the rough
> stop acting roughly or uncouthly

cut
> finished: the keg's cut; drunk:
> Mum's cut and the tea's ruined

cuz(zy), cuzzy-bro
> a term of address or reference
> used mainly among Maori

D

dag
an amusing character; a wag

Dally
a familiar, partially derogatory name for a 'Dalmatian', one whose ancestors emigrated from the Dalmatian coast of the former Yugoslavia

daylight robbery
said of exorbitant prices or gouging (e.g. bank) charges

de facto
of an interpersonal relationship, equivalent to legal marriage; a partner in such a relationship

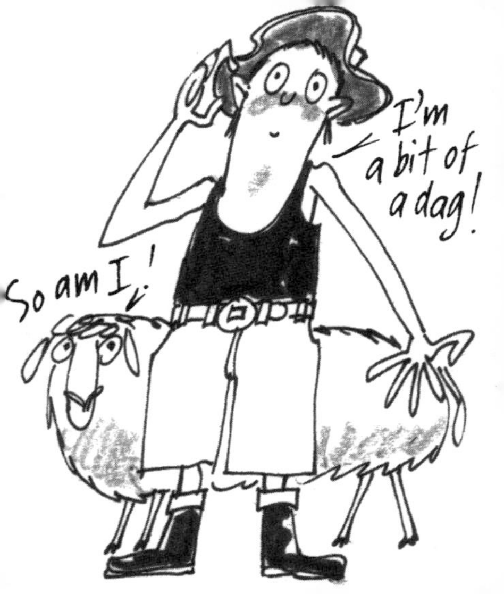
I'm a bit of a dag!
So am I!

deli
    a delicatessen

dig, Old Dig
    a (returned) serviceman; also
    used as a term of address

dill
    a fool or stupid person

dingbats
    crazy; *in the dingbats*, in a fit of
    delirium tremens

dinkum
    true, genuine, proper; *the
    dinkum oil*, correct information

dirty Turk
    rhyming slang for work

do one's block, bun, scone
> to lose control of one's emotional self

dob in
> the Kiwi game of reporting the peccadilloes of one's friends and neighbours to the authorities

dogbox
> as *in the dogbox,* in bad odour (with), in a place or attitude of penance

dole bludgers
> an offensive name for those on State support, especially those on family or unemployment benefits

doolan
  a Catholic

down the gurgler
  of plans, etc., failed completely

down to the wire
  of a contest, etc., excruciatingly
  closely contested

drongo
  a stupid fool

drop one's bundle
  to fart; to defecate; to become
  upset: e.g. at others' bundle-
  dropping

dunny
  a privy

dyke
  a privy (usually outdoor), a
  long-drop

E

earbash
to talk incessantly

earbasher
a person who steals the
conversation from others

ewesterer
a cross between a ewe and a
musterer

F

fair cow
of a person, thing or situation, abominable

fart sack
a polite term for a sleeping-bag, or bed

financial
having cash money

fit as a buck rat
very fit

fizz-boat
a small power-boat

flicks
movies, pictures

flog
to steal

fly cemetery
a fruit square, comprising dried
fruit between two pastry layers

flyblown
broke, unfinancial

footie
rugby union or league

full as a bull
very drunk

full as a tick
ditto

G

get stuck into
  to attack vigorously (a person, a problem, a piece of work)

get the willies
  be overcome with trepidation

get your a into g
  (arse into gear) hurry up!

gidday, g'die
  a commonly mumbled greeting

gink
  a bloke

give it a burl
  give it a try

go butchers (hook) at
  rhyming slang on *go crook at*, to
  go off at

go for the doctor
  make a supreme effort

go off pop at
  to scold

Godzone
  New Zealand as a post-Christian
  democracy: 'God's own country
  but the devil's own mess.'
  (Richard John Seddon, one-time
  Premier.)

goob
  a gob of phlegm, especially as
  ejected by sportspeople in the
  public eye

good on you
  said to encourage

good-oh
  a term of agreement

goorie
  a mongrel dog (from Maori *kuri*
  dog)

graunch
  to grind noisily, as of metal
  scraping a rough surface

greasies
  takeaways, especially fish and
  chips

grouse
  fine, excellent

H

handle
a 'pint' glass beer mug or its contents

happy as a flea on a dog
very happy

happy as Larry
ditto

hard case
an amusing or independent fellow; a rough diamond; a 'dag'

hard yacker
hard work

hash-foundry
a restaurant or eating-house

have gorse in one's pocket
  to be slow in paying one's share

head sherang
  the big chief

hoha
  fed up, tired; tiresome (from
  Maori *hoha* wearied)

holding
  having cash money

hollywood
  a faked or exaggerated injury to
  gain a rest or advantage on a
  sportsfield

home on the pig's back
  successful, well-off

hoon
> a lout; as a verb *to hoon around,* to indulge in loutish behaviour

hooray
> a Kiwi farewell

hophead
> a heavy drinker

hori
> an offensive word for a Maori

How would you be?
> a greeting, 'How are you?'

humdinger
> excellent, beaut; or something excellent of its kind; formerly said to be the bell that hung on the back of a nightcart

I

illegal Tegel
wild pigeon as food: pigeon is a protected species, 'Tegel' is the name of a popular brand of frozen chicken

in boots and all
said of a vicious attack or a vigorous rugby ruck

Irish curtains
cobwebs

BEGORAH THAT'S LOVELY KATHLEEN!

J

Joe (Hunt)
  a fool

joe blakes
  rhyming slang for snakes

john hop
  rhyming slang for cop (from
  original John (Dunn), a play on
  'gendarme')

joker
  a bloke: e.g. a good Kiwi joker
  is seldom amusing

K

kai kart
  a pie-cart often specialising in
  Maori foods such as pies and
  fish and chips

kapai
  good; often as an exclamation,
  from Maori

kero
  kerosene: often elsewhere called
  paraffin

kick up bobsidie
  to make a great fuss or noise

kiwi
a flightless bird; a New Zealand person; a rugby league representative

knuckle sandwich
a fist in the teeth

L

ladies a plate (or basket)
bring a contribution of food

lagerphone
a refined tambourine made of bottletops loosely nailed to a broomstick, a musical memorial to Kiwi ingenuity and taste

land-shark
a land speculator, a former name for a present curse

laughing gear
the teeth

lawyer
  a horrid thorny vine or bushy
  tangle from whose clutches a
  victim escapes only with
  difficulty and at great personal
  cost

leftfooter
  a Catholic

live on the smell of an oily rag
  to live frugally, as on the
  unemployment benefit

log of wood
  a familar name for the Ranfurly
  Shield, an interprovincial rugby
  trophy

lolly
  a sweet; *the lolly*, money

long acre
the grazing along the side of a
public road

loopie
a tourist

M

mad as a meat-axe
  very angry or crazy

make a sale
  to vomit

mate
  a familiar; also used as a term
  of address to strangers

micky doolan
  a Catholic

milkshake
  baking soda fed illicitly to
  racehorses as an aid to
  performance

mobster
  a member of the Mongrel Mob
  gang

Mong(rel)
ditto

mountain oyster
sheep's testicle eaten raw or
fricasseed by local eunuchs

muldoonery
the policies (especially economic) and abrasive personal style of a former Prime Minister, R.D. Muldoon

my oath!
indicating agreement or mild enthusiasm

mystery bag
a sausage or saveloy

N

naughty
 a coy Kiwism for a bout of
 sexual intercourse

ning-nong
 a failed no-hoper

no beg pardons
 said of a vigorous attack

no fear
 indicating refusal or
 disagreement

no flies on
 said of a smart or shrewd
 person: often to a freckled
 person tagged 'but you can see
 where they've been'

no hoper
    a confirmed failure

North Cape to the Bluff
    from one end of New Zealand
    to the other

not much chop
    not very useful or advantageous

not the full quid
    mentally deficient, not 'all there'

not to have a (brass) razoo
    to be broke

not to know one's arse from one's elbow
    to be thoroughly confused or
    ignorant

not to know someone from a bar of soap
    not to recognise

**not to know whether one is
Arthur or Martha**
    to be totally confused or stupid

not worth tin of fish
    of little worth

O

OE, overseas experience
the fledgling Kiwi's mandatory trip to Europe

off they go says Bob Munro
a rhyming tag associated with starting races or losing appendages, etc.

offsider
the assistant of another, especially of a cook

old identity
one who has lived long in one place; often termed 'old nonentity'

oldie
a parent, or other aged person, especially one able to wield grey power

one out of the box
said of anything fine or outstanding, especially of a fine day

on one's pat (malone)
rhyming slang for on one's own

on the box seat
in a situation of advantage

on the never-never
on time payment

open slather
a free-for-all

P

Parrie
a familiar name for
Paremoremo, a maximum
security prison

pavlova, pav
a New Zealand meringue
pudding with a fruit and cream
filling used as a dessert tease
for weight-watchers

perve
to stare or ponder lustfully

peter
a till or cash-register; also a
beer-flagon

pie cart
    a mobile cart selling meals and takeaway foods

Pig Islands
    New Zealand, from the number of resident swine

Pig Islander
    a New Zealander

piker
    one who fails in obligations; a coward

pisshead
    a heavy drinker

plastic fantastic
    a New Zealand name for a loser in a yacht race

plonk
    liquor, especially cheap wine

poke the borax (or borak)
    to chaff or tease

pom(mie)
    a Britisher, formerly *homie*

Pongolia
    Mother England

poofter
    in old-fashioned speech, a skite
    or blowhard

poor cow
    an unfortunate or miserable
    person

possie, pozzie
    a position, a place of advantage

pressie
> a present

prez
> president, especially a gang president

puckeroo
> to break, ruin: from Maori *pakaru*, broken

puku
> stomach: from Maori *puku*, stomach

pull a fastie
> to put across a clever, usually dishonest, stroke

pull a swiftie
> ditto

put one's pot on
   to report to the authorities, to
   dob in

put the boot in
   to punish severely, especially an
   opponent who is down or weak

Q

quack
    a medical doctor

Queen Street farmer
    a businessman owning rural
    property: from the name of
    Auckland's main street

R

rafferty('s) rules
  no rules at all

rapt
  extremely pleased

rare as rocking-horse shit
  very rare

ratbag
  an untrustworthy person, a rogue

rattle one's dags
  to hurry up: from the noise
  of dry dags rattling as
  sheep are driven along

repo man
  a repossession
  agent

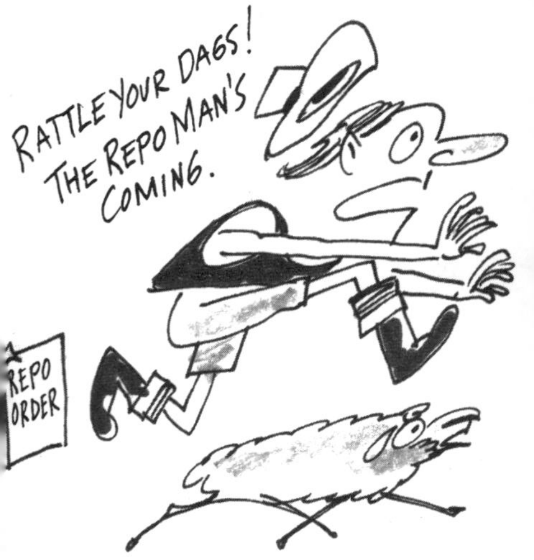

RATTLE YOUR DAGS!
THE REPO MAN'S
COMING.
REPO
ORDER

rigger
   a beer-flagon

ring-bolt
   to travel illicitly in a ship, hidden
   in the crews' quarters

ringer
   an expert

rip, shit, or bust
   a phrase indicating
   determination to finish a project
   regardless of the result

Rogernomics
   an economic miracle played on
   an unsuspecting public

root
   to enforce sexual intercourse on
   a person

ropeable
   very angry

rough as guts
   roughly made or turned out;
   uncouth

rouseabout
   one who does various kinds of
   unskilled manual work

rubberty-dub, rub-a-dub, rubbity
   rhyming slang for pub

rustbucket
   a decrepit motor vehicle

S

scarce as hens' teeth
very scarce

scroggin
a tramper's high energy food of
mixed dried fruit, nuts, etc.

scunge
a nasty, dirty, greasy person;
hence *scungy*, applied to such
people and things

send her down Hughie
an invocation to rain: Hughie is
the highly effable name of a
local *Jupiter Pluvialis*

session
> a drinking bout with
> acquaintances

sexo
> a person oversexed but
> underpinned

she's or she'll be apples, jake, right
> it's all right, okay

sheila
> a girl(friend); a woman

shickered
> drunk: from Yiddish *shicker*,
> drunk

ship-girl
> a prostitute working ships

shook on
  keen on, attracted to

shoot through
  to leave suddenly

shout
  to treat; a treat, especially of liquor

shrewdie
  a shrewd trick; a clever or tricky person

shufti
  a look (at something)

sickie
  a period of sick-leave from work, often caused by Mondayitis

silly as a two-bob watch
  very silly

sink the boot in
to kick viciously, especially an opponent who is down

sit up like jacky
to sit up straight (and take notice); to sit up with obvious confidence

six-o'clock closing
a former method of insisting drunks go home for tea

six-o'clock swill
the Kiwi drinking scene during the time when hotel bars were closed at six o'clock

skerrick
a small piece, especially as 'not a skerrick left'

skinner
finished, empty: 'The food's a skinner.'

skinnier than a gumdigger's dog
very skinny

skite
to boast; boasting

skull
to sink beer quickly, especially in a drinking contest: from Scandinavian *skol*, a toast

slinter
a devious trick or stratagem

slushy
a kitchen rouseabout or cook's offsider

smoko, smoke-oh
 a refreshment break from work

snaky
 of nasty or uncertain temper

snarler
 sausage

snivelling snufflebuster
 an old-fashioned name for a
 moaner or whinger

snork
 a baby or young child

sook(ie)
 a crybaby, a cowardly child; also
 a calf or a call to a calf

southerly buster
 a violent southerly gale

spieler
   a fast-talker; a con-man

square-rigger
   a flat-sided square bottle
   originally holding 'square' gin

squiz
   a look: 'Gissa squiz atya snork.'

stair-dancer
    a thief whose beat is
    multi-storey office buildings

**stand off the grass (and let my
wife see the races)**
    said to a person blocking one's
    view

steam
    methylated spirits as a street
    drink

steinie
    a small bottle of Steinlager
    brand lager as a bar drink

stickybeak
    an inquisitive person; to behave
    in an inquisitive way

stirrer
> a polite form of *shit-stirrer,* a trouble-maker

stone the crows
> an exclamation of surprise or mild disbelief

stonkered
> beaten, brought to a standstill

stoush
> a fight, a brawl; brawling

swiftie
> a shrewd or dishonest trick or gambit

T

tall *poppy*
>an outstanding person ripe for
cutting down by inferiors or by
the Kiwi-clobbering machine

tangi
>a party; from *tangi*, a Maori
funeral ceremony

Taranaki gate
>a makeshift gate of wire and
battens

tart
>a woman, seldom loose

technicolour yawn
>a multi-coloured vomiting

the demons, the dees
    detectives

the Other Side
    Australia

thick as pigshit
    of a person, exceedingly
    brainless

Think Big
    a name given to public policies
    and works whose cost exceeds
    their uselessness

tickle the peter
    to take money from the till
    regularly

**tight as a duck's arse (and
that's watertight)**
    said of a person mean with
    money

till the cows come home
indicating a longish period with no promise of success at the end of it: You can cry till the cows come home, but you're not watching the late programme.

...he duff
pregnant

up the wop
awry; pregnant

use a five-fingered chequebook
to steal or shoplift

I SHOULD'VE USED A CONDOM!

tinny
    lucky

tinpot
    often of a place, small, insignificant

to *chat* someone
    to give corrective advice; put a person in the kn[ow]

toby
    the mains stopcock co[ntrolling] water delivery to prope[rty]; from Scottish dialect

toey
    excitable; on edge; fas[t] mark

town bike
    a person free with sex

V

vegies
    vegetables

MOO

W

Were you born in a tent?
    said to a person leaving a door open

whole shooting-box
    everything or everyone; the 'whole box of tricks'

Whykickamookau
an imaginary place, whose form
parodies that of Maori
place-names

widgie
    a subcultural female of the 1950s

within cooee of
    within reach of; *not to come
    within coo-ee of,* to come
    nowhere near a goal

woop-woops, wop-wops
    usually, *up* or *in the wop-wops,*
    the remote areas

wowser
    a puritanical spoilsport; one
    who disapproves of pleasures
    other than her or his own

Y

yahoo
 to act the lout in a noisy fashion

you can put a ring round that
 indicating a strong affirmative
 emphasis

z

zambuck

a first aid person of the Order of
St John, especially when
attending a sports gathering:
from the name of a
once-popular brand of ointment
Zambuk

First published 1992 by Reed Books,
a division of Reed Publishing (NZ) Ltd,
39 Rawene Road, Birkenhead, Auckland 10.
Associated companies, branches and representatives
throughout the world.

Reprinted 1993

ISBN 0 7900 0272 8

Designed by Geoff Hocking
Typeset by DigiType
Produced in Australia by The Five Mile Press
Printed in Singapore by Tien Wah Press